About Kindness

BY Jacy Lee

Dedication

This book is dedicated to my beloved Mother
who taught me kindness, and to all my young
grandnieces, grandnephews and godchildren
who make me smile.

Find the Heart

This **red heart** is embedded in each of the illustrations. As you read, I invite you to find the heart in each illustration and think about whether you have received similar acts of kindness from someone and whether you have done similar acts of kindness for someone else.

When you **receive** kindness from someone, how does that act of kindness make you feel? When you **do** an act of kindness for someone, how does it make you feel?

An act of kindness can bring **good** and **positive** feelings for the recipient and the doer, and it can also lead to **another** act of kindness. Would you try to do one random act of kindness daily?

Kindness is taking care in all you do,
Thinking of people's needs and helping too.

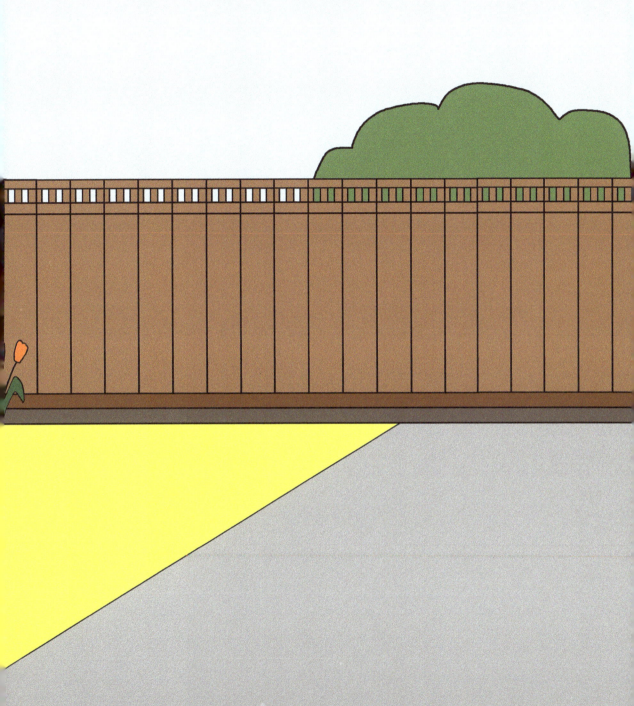

Lending a hand with household chores.

Sharing your umbrella when it pours.

Helping a person cross the street safely.

Standing up for someone teased by a bully.

Carrying a person's load that looks heavy.

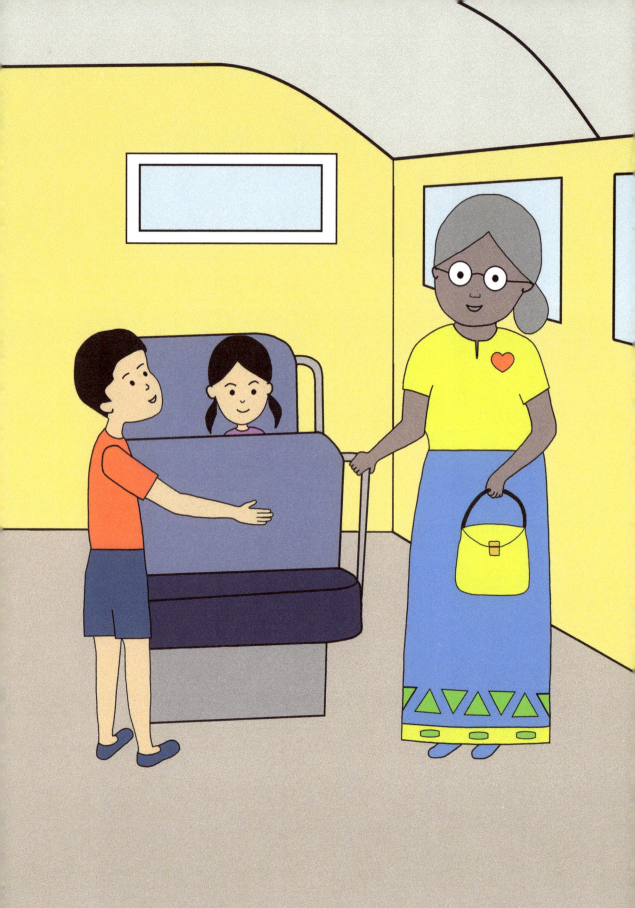

Offering your seat to someone weary.

Kindness is taking care in all you do,
Understanding people's feelings and being true.

When someone is lonely, say "hello" warmly.

When they are sad, hug them gently.

When they are angry, listen calmly to them.

When they cry out of fear, offer what help you can.

When they are hungry, share your food willingly.

When they win an award, share their joy without envy.

**Kindness is taking care in all you do,
Caring for your community and planet too.**

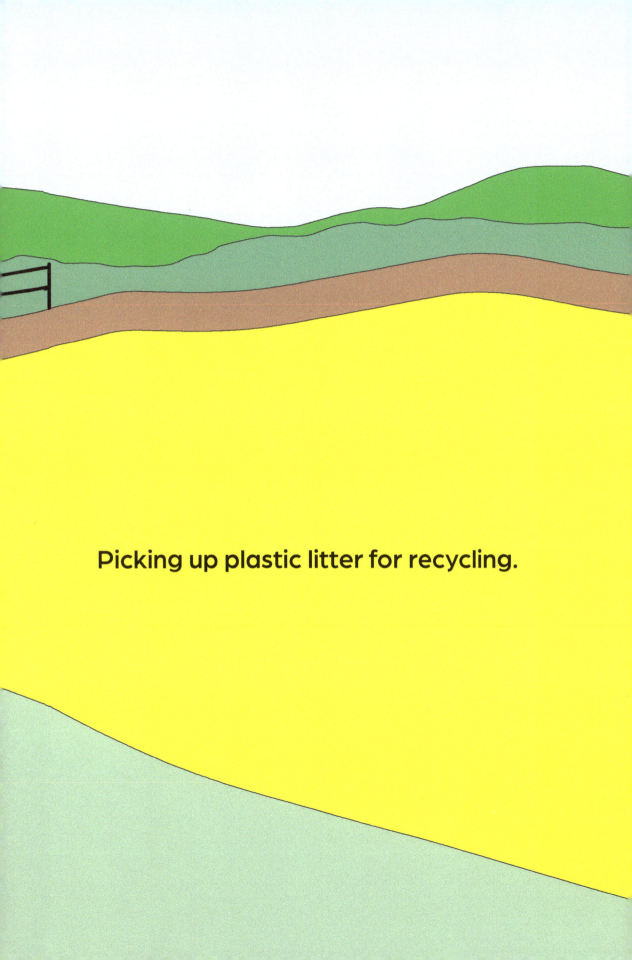

Picking up plastic litter for recycling.

Planting young trees to keep the world green.

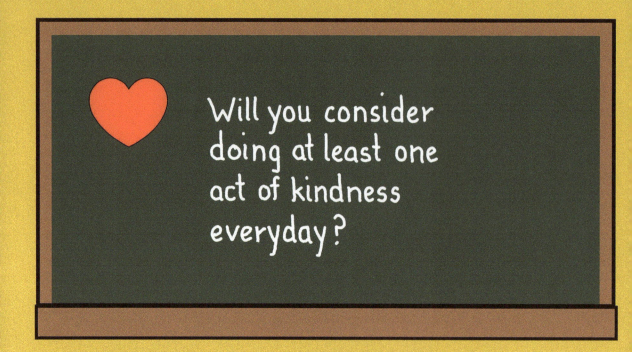

Will you consider doing at least one act of kindness everyday?

Acting in kindness without wanting reward,
Inspires people to pass on kindness abroad.

Kindness spreads and brings happiness and unity,
Togetherness in diversity, and
love among humanity.

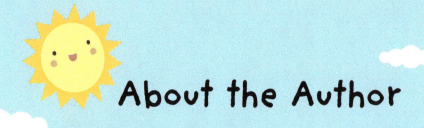

About the Author

Victoria-based author Jacy Lee cares about and believes in the power of kindness. Believing that there can be no such thing as too much kindness, she decided to write and illustrate a short verse book on the topic to help young children understand what kindness is and how it can make a positive impact in the world. Her hope is that the children who read and re-read her book, or have it read to them, will not only practise kindness during their childhood but throughout their life.

Jacy recently retired from a career in educational leadership and policy, and now devotes her time to caring for her elderly mother. She also volunteers in various capacities, including as a volunteer counsellor at a counselling centre, and as a community representative on a local government committee. Her educational background includes a Master of Law from the University of Cambridge, and a Doctor of Education from the University of British Columbia. She is also the proud godmother and aunt to many lucky children.

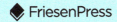

FriesenPress

One Printers Way
Altona, MB R0G0B0,
Canada

www.friesenpress.com

ISBN
978-1-03-911941-3 (Hardcover)
978-1-03-911940-6 (Paperback)
978-1-03-911942-0 (eBook)

1. JUVENILE NONFICTION, POETRY

Distributed to the trade by The Ingram Book Company

CPSIA information can be obtained
at www.ICGtesting.com
Printed in the USA
BVHW020516080222
628342BV00001B/1

9 781039 119406